The Places I've Been

Darina Jean

BookLeaf Publishing

Presentation by *BookLeaf Publishing*

Web: www.bookleafpub.com

E-mail: info@bookleafpub.com

ISBN: 9789357443128

First edition 2023

I'd like to dedicate this book to the people who are always so strong but don't always have a voice.

ACKNOWLEDGEMENT

I wouldn't be anywhere without a mom who always reminded me that the only person that can keep me down is myself. Who instilled in me to dream big and I'll be bigger than my dreams. I'm eternally grateful for the loves and friends I've had that have given me the best experiences and lessons life has to offer.

PREFACE

Fuck. I'm sad enough to write again.

The White House

My biggest fear is opening up
Only for them to decide
That they don't like the color of my bones
That the lines in my brain aren't drawn the right way
That my curves are all wrong and crooked
I fear that if they open up my book
They won't like how I read
Because I am not a simple bow tied novel glued neatly together
So I present myself as a redacted legal document without a spine
Telling only what needs to be known
Hiding all the dirty
And all the gritty

The Black Sea

I feel like an open Black Sea
My eyes could tell you that
Shit brown so dark
You wouldn't know one pupil is bigger than the other,
If I didn't tell you that
Even with the warmth of the sun
The water won't run.

The Crime

My apologies
If my loving you
Ever hurt you
It was a crime of passion

The Trees

I envy trees and the way they live
Touching the sky and the earth

The Home

The home is on fire.
It keeps me warm
Outside is flooded.
I never thirst
The earth shakes.
I know how to hide and save myself
No need to call emergency services
With a touch like Midas, I'm good in a crisis

The Body

I've been to your body
I know what it likes
I've touched how it feels
And I've climbed in inside
I've listened to your heartbeats
Then I gave you mine
But deep in your stomach
Something was eating you alive,
Because you knew what I couldn't
Deep in your bones.
I've been to your body
But I could never get inside your mind

The Place I Found Myself

The place I found myself
Was unexpected.
Wrong for what I don’t know
Distraught from what I do
Oh this must be a test
To my humanity
Or so I thought
But I must’ve passed.
The place I found myself
Was unexpected.
Right where I started

The Route/ Mind

I talk so happy but write so sad, why?
Maybe I haven't found the right song to sing and dance in my mind
Maybe the thoughts aren't always so kind
Maybe there's a secret darkness that rules the inside
Perhaps.
But maybe I just needed to let these things out
Things I wouldn't dare let slip from my mouth
So these ashes can fall and I can take a new route

The Desert

Juicy lips
Juicy hips
Even with the dip
I know you'd like to dip on in
Learn what makes me shine and my darkest sins
Well truth is, I walk like sunshine
Because I stood in the sun rays and let it bathe
me in fire
I let it wash away then reignite my desire
And that's why you keep me like Hestia
Right next to ya
Because I keep ya fire
I keep you warm
I keep dying and being reborn
I'm no Messiah
I've just hit the ground like Gaia
I've just been thru the desert like Himalayas
And still.
Juicy

The Beach

Gold mends a broken heart
Golden yellow Yukon potatoes that she plates with her steak
Golden sun rays on solo beach days
I could get used to this
Five gold stars
Light my eyes up, staring at the sun
No tears fall.
Because gold mends a broken heart
When you realize you are golden
And all you have to do is pour gold like cement into the gaping hole that was left
From all that you missed

The Wishing Well

The other night I found myself at a wishing well
Where I dreamed of all the things that could—
should, would be
In the moonlight I saw a reflection of a home
instead of a hotel
I saw all the ways that I have misunderstood me

The next morning the sun tattooed my scars gold
I did all the things that I couldn't— shouldn't,
wouldn't
And to be frank I have never felt more consoled
And for once I didn't care how they told it

I had had the plan for us that night at the wishing
well
Instead I chose just to wish you well

The Flame

Oh love come on in
Before I was scared of the fire
But now I play with the flame
Drunken on this pain
Hurting with this wine
This little light of mine
Is most-definitely going to shine
But it can't rain.
Someone remembers I like candles
I love the warmth
But sometimes I hate the heat
I love the way it smells
So I guess the favor lies in my desires
Sometimes I stop the music
And take a beat
To listen to what's in between
And I don't hear much
But I feel everything
It makes me woozy
The way these vibrations move me
Yet a tear falls
And i feel nothing
Numb drunk
Tomorrow I'll win
So love come on in

I miss the heat
Because before I was scared of the fire
But now I play with the flame
Somewhere along where I learned your name

The Warmth

I long to press my bones against a body
Fully dressed but still bare
I want to hug somebody
But I want the kind of hug that feels like you're being held
You know like held and hidden away from all the dangers of the world?
Between flesh that feels more like home than a human
The kind where you're warm,
Wrapped up in a blanket
Cuddled up on your bed with a good book
Mm his sweet scent like a candle there to light me up and keep me warm.
The kind of hug I guess you'd call a warm embrace
For it embraces all of your fears, tears, and tears
Just the thought of it
Turns my insides into caramel
Warm

What I'm searching for must be

Warm.?

The Box

I’m vulnerable
I’m real
I’m raw
From trying
And also from not trying
And maybe even a little tired
Tired because my nails are worn down from all the scratching I’ve done
In my desperate need to make it out of the box
Fingers bloody because I don’t know who I am
Just what I’ve been
And what I could be, or want to be, or wish to be

The Sound

Oh my goodness
Has it always been this loud
How could they ever sleep with sound
I used it to cover up my tears
Even used it up on all of my fears
That no one else but me can feel
But still I feel
How could they ever sleep with this sound
Has it always been so loud
Hmm anyways I've turned it down
It's reserved only for me now
It's no longer lonely to me now
I know you wish to see how
I've cracked my back
And readied my spine
Read between the lines

The Solid Matter

If these walls could talk
They would scream
If these walls could walk
They would run
But they're paralyzed in here
Guess you have to be solid to be strong

The Challenge

He likes when I write
It makes him feel something
A little human.
He likes the way I paint my thoughts
Cus I can never be simple, always a little bit of a challenge.
Thinks I should be in a book or something
I probably will if I ever stop writing about him

The Crowds

I wonder when they see me
Do they see just a pretty face
And a little waist

Or do they see
Just another heart to break
A body to ravage

Drowning in the crowds of those who love me
Screaming for someone to notice me
So everyone
And even me
Can see that I exist

The Kind

I'm kind not nice
Because I no longer care to be digestible
I don't need you to feel desirable
Because every time I've given myself on a plate
to you
You took me in
Took my nutrients and vitamins
Thanked me for what I did not who I am
Then shit me out without a thought again
So I am kind
Because I've seen your guts and your mind
I've seen the hurt you hide behind
I see the way you've been living to survive
So I am kind
Because I understand
What it's like to lose the upper hand
Going through life without a plan
And feeling like no one can
Be kind

The Strong

What didn't kill me never made me stronger
I was already strong
It made me realize all that I could reconquer

The Sun

I found a place in the sun
It started with me needing a place to run

www.ingramcontent.com/pod-product-compliance
Lightning Source LLC
Chambersburg PA
CBHW051758130826
49812CB00033B/1201
9789357443128